Portrait of an Artist as a Young Poseur
Boston 1974 to 1983

By Doug Holder

ISBN: 978-0-9908413-6-4

Printed in the United States of America
By Big Table Publishing Company
Boston, MA

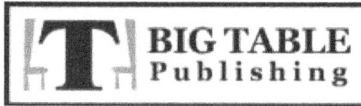

T BIG TABLE Publishing

Cover Photo: *271 Newbury Street* by Shan Achhiwala ©2010 courtesy of Shabunawaz Photography

Also by Doug Holder:

Poetry
Eating Grief at 3:00 a.m.
Poems from the Left Bank
The Man in the Booth in the Midtown Tunnel
Of All the Meals I Had Before
No One Dies at the Au Bon Pain
Wrestling with my Father
Dreams at the Au Bon Pain
Waking in a Cold Sweat
Poems of Boston and Just Beyond

Non-Fiction
From the Paris of New England: Interviews with Poets and Writers
Louisa Solano: The Grolier Poetry Book Shop

Reviews

"Doug Holder is a poet of the old city, the city of our fathers, of the 1950s and later. Mr. Holder writes poems like notes in a diary. I found myself struck by their economy, wit, and urban melancholy... He has a voice unlike that of any of his contemporaries. Holder is a poet of the street and coffeehouses, an observer of the everyday. He writes of old Marxists, security guards and his relationship to his deceased father—themes of the common life. I am drawn to these poems as I am to the poetry of Philip Levine and the prose of James T. Farrell. But Holder's poetry is deeper than that. He sees the world not for what it is, but on his own terms. He is living in the poem rather than in poetry."
~ Sam Cornish, First Boston Poet Laureate

"This book is a jewel; multifaceted, scintillating, and completely unique. There is not a wasted word within the covers of this printed gift... instead, a complete, complex text pointillism capturing the era and place perfectly. If you lived within a thousand miles of the scene when it was happening, you will smile more than once at the memories of things long forgotten. Do yourself a favor and buy one for a loved one's future present."
~ Christopher Reilley, *Breathing for Clouds* and *Grief Tattoos*

"Doug Holder's *Portrait of an Artist as a Young Poseur* has the immediacy of film, pulling the reader in: 'I lived in a room on the top floor ($38/week), bathroom down the hall–a stairway to the roof–cockroaches...' The writing is pointed, unpretentious and honest, providing snapshots of rough-edged jobs and unvarnished people, places in Boston that have vanished, historical snippets on the street, in restaurants and subways. Whether he's describing experience as a young man, or painting transience itself, the writing feels sensitive and authentic, something to read and reread."
~ Nina R. Alonso, Founding Editor of *Constellations Magazine*

"The echoes of Doug Holder's footsteps are felt in this exploration of Boston and his nascent self. With reflective humor, he unfolds moments of insight amid vernal uncertainty. The vignettes are enticing, fondly resonating time and place."
~ Richard Fox, *Time Bomb: Poems*

"*Portrait of an Artist as a Young Poseur* is a unique memoir, in poetry, of a real Boston artist looking back at a distinct point in time at a city I love. The man, the city, the book are all completely unique, wonderful and original."
~ Timothy Gager, *The Thursday Appointments of Bill Sloan*

"Doug Holder writes about the old Boston, before the city changed, before gentrification. With a knack for storytelling, he brings to life, all the characters who crossed his path from 1974-1983, while living in Boston. This book is humorous, charming and Holder's descriptions are intriguing of city life at that time. This is a film waiting to be made."
~ Gloria Mindock, Červená Barva Press

"What can be said of someone who has lived such a life as described in this book, where no person, place or situation is considered off-limits, where the everyday is invoked as a kind of miracle— such a person being Doug Holder: poet, teacher, publisher, editor, interviewer and advocate of writers and writing. *Portrait of an Artist as a Young Poseur* is a stunning read."
~ Susan Tepper, *The Merrill Diaries* and *From the Umberplatzen*

For Jim Resnick

Table of Contents

Introduction

Recently one of my Facebook friends from Minnesota posted that she'd met someone who was from Boston. "I know a poet from Boston," my friend told the woman, "his name is Doug Holder. Do you know him?" The woman's response was, "Everyone knows Doug Holder." When I read the Facebook post, it occurred to me that if I had to choose one phrase to describe Doug Holder it would be *Everyone knows him*. I would also add *Everyone respects him* and *Everyone loves him*. Truly, the bio in the back of this elegant little book doesn't do justice to all his accomplishments.

My history with him goes back to 2007, when I came up with the idea to contact McLean Hospital (a mental health facility) and suggest I do writing workshops with the people living there. But when I called I was told, "Sorry, we already have someone doing that. You probably know him – Doug Holder." I didn't at that point, but I did recognize the name when just a few months later this Doug Holder person submitted a poem to me at *Boston Literary Magazine*. I snapped it up at once.

After that, I kept hearing about him. The more involved I became in the local writing scene, the more his name came up in conversation; how could it not? He was everywhere–editor of Ibbetson Street Press, arts editor of his city's newspaper, writing instructor at not one but two colleges, and author of several collections of poetry. Timidly, I sent him a friend request, and he accepted. Then to my shock, he invited me to be on his show *Poet to Poet* in January of 2012, and at last we met face to face. I expected to feel intimidated and shy, but his warmth and humor immediately put me at ease. A year later he asked if I would be a feature at his Newton Library poetry series, an event he hosts once a month during the spring, summer, and fall, for the sole purpose of giving poets a chance to read to a crowd. These were huge for me, and no amount of e mails saying "thank you" and posting those little hearts by typing "<" and "3" on his wall could even begin to express my gratitude to him for including me in both of these series.

Our relationship came full circle in March of 2015 when he approached me at Big Table Publishing Company to ask if he could submit a manuscript. I accepted it without even seeing it. I also told him that I had been planning to call him and let him know that The Newton Writing and Publishing Center board of directors had just unanimously voted for him to be the first recipient of our Allen Ginsberg Literary Community Contribution Award. If ever there was a "no brainer," choosing him was one!

When I read *Portrait of an Artist as a Young Poseur*, I felt an instant connection with these snapshots of a young man avoiding convention as he navigates the tricky waters of fashion, poetry, romance, and rueful self-awareness.

I, too, had moved to Massachusetts in the early 70s, and recall the Boston of those years, and the iconic places he describes here with his wonderfully edgy grace. I remember being scandalized by the items in the window of Jack's Joke Shop. I remember watching Kirby Perkins on the channel 5 news. Kens' Deli–yes, I used to go there late at night with my girlfriends once we learned to drive. I like to think that if I'd run into him there, we would have met, chatted... and then I could have said "Of course I know Doug Holder!" years ago.

Robin Stratton
Boston, MA

Prologue

This long, stream of consciousness poem concerns my early years in Boston. It is a sort of dream-like memoir, of a young man trying to realize a dream, even when the dream was not fully formulated. During those years I was a boy trying on different men's suits; I was an Adonis of posturing and mimicking. But in some ways that hapless creature that was me, I admire and love. And that's because he didn't follow the standard course of college, graduate school, marriage, house, family, but drifted in search of something, something just out of reach, never to be fully realized. In those years I was a true romantic in my own way, a poor man's Don Quixote; a time I remember with a bit of embarrassment and a tender smile.

Doug Holder
Somerville, Mass.
2015

Part 1: Newbury Street

I lived at 271 Newbury Street from 1978 to 1983 shortly after I graduated from college, in a room on the top floor ($38/week), bathroom down the hall—a stairway to the roof—cockroaches—above *Davio's* Restaurant. I worked at the Fatted Calf in Copley Square as a short order cook, and sold the *Globe* over the phone in Cambridge. Used to frequent the Exeter Theatre down the block—Marx Brothers, *Rocky Horror*—chanting at midnight—ate at Guild's Drugstore across from the Lenox Hotel. Ethel, the counterwoman, kept up a continuous narrative of her rotten kids in the Old Colony project in Southie... I was an assistant manager at Big L Discounts for a stint—health and beauty aids, can you believe it?... taught in the South End at Dr. Solomon Carter Mental Health Center—DYS-DSS kids... field trips to Roxbury and the abandoned Jewish temples... home visits for the kids... the families smoking pot and doing lines. There was a restaurant I used to frequent, the Peter Piper on Beacon Street. Big cafeteria-style food, poetry readings. Jim and I sat near the steam table, our words floating on a mist of steamed cabbage—and I was habitually at the Kebab and Curry... sitar and sag. I used to see Richard Yates (*Revolutionary Road),* a drunken shamble down the block, and I had the same Chinese laundry as talk radio host David Brudnoy (The Chinese man always used to yell at me *Why you lose ticket?*) Brudnoy, his pockmarked and intelligent face, with an ironic smile. I worked as a clerk at the corner of Newbury and Beacon Street, Sunny Corner Farms. Members of the Cars used to come in regularly—Rick so sky high, fingering a Twinkie... also Gilda Rudner—a frenzy of frenzied hair, Howard Zinn—tall, a radical patrician, and Barney Frank—rumpled and in a rush—all on the night shift. And beers after work at Frankenstein's. My boss, a fat Irishman, called me *dirty kike* regularly after he had a few... nice to me the next day. I remember the ancient, gay security guard—Maynard—he used to come to chat—and always told me stories how young, virile men were enamored with him, his guard hat tilted at a rakish angle—oh, but he pleaded that he maintained his purity. And the toothless whore who only gave head to her man—her point of honor. And during a snowstorm I gave shelter to the street icon, Mr. Butch... almost left him in the store overnight... the Victor Hugo bookshop—what a joint—cloistered myself with the used and rare... and the Newbury Steak House —remember the chef—black dude, a real card—dirty jokes and hard-earned wisdom—we used to shoot the shit. I even had a sort of girlfriend—well—later learned she was community property, if you know what I mean. I remember sitting on the stoop of my brownstone on a hot summer night, and people would stop and chat—shoot the breeze. And I was dead drunk and I asked the drunks sleeping on the warm air of the grates by the Boston Public Library what the meaning of life was—they told me: *Fuck off*. That thick mound of hash and eggs that I devoured every morning, and Malaba, the Zimbabwe-man on the night shift at McLean—rasping in his Louis Armstrong voice, calling it Hashish Browns , would be dead if I continued that habit. Those nights writing in my furnished room, the clank, clank of the radiator—thinking I was a Beat poet or something. The mice scurried by—my father told me, over the phone: *Get the hell out of there!* My mother joined in, *That's the lifestyle they lead, Larry*. Hordes of us made the pilgrimage to be with the rodents and roaches… all-night poker games with the service bartender who worked at the Hilton… the dishwashers from his shift, Latinos with flashy gold-filling smiles. Bartending was not his life he told us—he was going back to U/Mass Boston—for the past 5 years he told us.

Part 2: Father's, The North End

Oh that distinct flushed-out smell of Father's Five—tattooed, Hell's Angels, ready to bounce you at the door—the Citgo sign flashing in the canyon of Kenmore Square… a signpost… direction… an elixir to your fog—vinyls *at* Looney Tunes—the old ladies of Coolidge Corner in Brookline who brought you their dead husbands' shirts when you manned the counter—*This should fit you,* they crooned. And you would be a walking monument to the dead. Cutting through the alleys in the Back Bay—a buffet in the trash bins for the down and out—they delicately picked at the remains of the day, sewage and rot behind tony shops—it was always Doomsday on the Common—street preachers at a clearance sale—street singers—songs for change—begging for it. The old Italian guy who yelled at you at the Haymarket: *Hey Kid, ripe tomatahs, get one for yer tomatah.* Laughing, the stub of a cigar shaking outside his mouth. The Mass. Ave. Bridge… it gave your life a horizon—open space from the small furnished room. My city on the hill—Buzzy's Roast Beef—a knish-delish—hotdog—oh, red phallus of beef, melts in my teeth. Karen, the Jewish girl I met at the matzo ball, we danced, and coupled in her small, flat in the North End. You learned how to love and leave—Caruso music and the couple that had operatic fights in sync… Her last words before she threw you out: *I can't stand all this eating!* Smell of bread baking all night on Salem Street—corpulent men outside the social club—called you *twinkle toes*—as you jogged by on chicken legs. Your friend—a clerk—dating a dwarf—an adjunct at Boston College—American Studies—a small love affair…

Part 3: Park Drive

Lived on Park Drive. Sounds fancy—but overlooked the subway tracks and the vast Sear's warehouse—the roar of the subway, the gray, looming Sears trucks in the distance—the trickle of the Muddy River. My window open—forgot I was nude—catcalls from the subway platform at my flabby body—bloated from the 11 to 7AM shift at McLean—sitting watching the 4-point restraints on patients—-rise and fall—with sedated breath. I saw so many of those chests: inflated, defeated, and deflated. The croissants from the Savoy Bakery in Audubon Circle were flaky concessions, the dark beers and the dark, cavernous bar at Browns, my balm. And the elevated tracks on Harrison Avenue—elevated me—I was a transcendent blur crosstown. The Dudley Bus idling near the vacant lot, rats as big as cats foraging near a fence. Sometimes I met her at the Nickelodeon… was it *Kiss of the Spiderwoman*? Held her hand, traced it the way I would trace her body later in the studio—a rail-thin graphic artist from Providence—she wrote me beautiful letters that made me swoon in my room.

Part 4: Combat Zone, Greyhound Bus Station, Boston Public Library

The Greyhound Station was near a Rockabilly Bar—the flashing, seductive light of the Playboy Club, hawked long legs and short resumes—I weaved my way to the carnality of the Combat Zone—down LaGrange Street. First stopping by Hand the Hatter, an avuncular old man—some fish—some fish out of order—water—in the midst of this—presiding over blocked, buffed, and august fedoras—the kind my father wore—his heels pounding the floors in Penn. Station. And the whore in the bar said: *Give this kid a glass of milk.* And all my street-wise posturing melted with these succinct words—not a boilermaker but a milk boy.

In the old wing of the Boston Public Library, Bacchante and Baby met me—lifting her child with joy—I wonder if my mother ever did that with me? A bust of Henry James stared at me at Bates Hall as I made my way to the Periodical Room—scrolls of newspapers—old men—half glasses, canes. I wondered why that man was praying over an *Anchorage Times*—the room smelled like sweat, vaguely ruinous—reading a rag—a waiting room for death.

Part 5: Fernald School, Malden

I met her at a school for the retarded—a working class girl—post Judge Tauro—we treated retarded women—trying to stop them from slapping feces on their clothes and ours—chaperoning them at a Fellini-like dance, men and women with gnarled hands, twisted legs, spittle drooling down from the sides of their mouths, partners—cheek to cheek. And they smiled, despite it all, *Oh yes, we all need love, we all need intimacy,*—I told myself—even when they threw food in our faces. Her name I forget—she took me to her parents' home in Malden—and being the snot I was—I felt superior—but I loved the way her tight body fell into mine when we danced—intoxicated with her perfume, loving her full red lipstick lips, her tough but girlish accent. We danced at the VFW hall—me with patched sports coat, and unruly bohemian beard. Italian union men looking at me like I was a strange bird—*faggot* under their breath. She drifted away—she said she couldn't understand me… nor could I.

Part 6: 271 Newbury Street

Early in the morning—I heard the retired Irish civil servant… a pensioner with a stained undershirt and plaid boxers—coughing up phlegm—heard through the thin walls: *How are you, me boy?* he crooned at me in the morning—both of us jockeying for the head down the hall. Then the fire alarm—a gas main break—out in the street—explosions traversed Newbury Street. I ran down the stairs in my blue corduroy sports jacket—a slightly irregular affair—from the depths of Filene's Basement… padded shoulders to bolster my narrow ones and a frail ego—a waxed mustache—the guys in the real estate office on the first floor used to crack: *Well, Hello Dali!* I made my way down the winding staircase (the spinster on the second floor opened the door a crack—she knew she would be flushed out)—me—with a red scarf around my skinny neck—like a poor man's ascot—Kirby Perkins, the newsman on the scene—I heard him say from the side of his mouth to the cameraman: *Look at this fuckin' character.* So oblivious to my absurdity—a beret on my already thinning hair—a rakish angle—I could be a posturing mannequin in one of the shop windows—central casting-clichéd young Beatnik.

Part 7: Copley Square, Ken's Deli

Copley Square—Midnight—slipped into Ken's Deli. A Jackie Gleasonish fat man—the manager—stationed by the rotisserie chickens—a chorus line of spread legs, melting flesh, wings posturing on their plump hips—wondering which one would I choose. A dishwasher emerged, effeminate man, dirty apron, a cigarette in a holder, long expressive hands, wearing an eye patch. Drag Queens in the men's room. At the counter on the first floor— a waitress—not long on patience piped: *What's it going to be, hon*. Actors off from a gig at the Colonial, gesturing to each other dramatically at the booths—a few years before—I was a dishwasher here. I was chosen from a lineup of world-weary men: *You, you and you*, at 5PM—peering at all this through stacks of dishes—all this would be mine one day—a late night character—laughing over corn beef and chopped liver on dark rye—with poets and writers, after a day of writing—joking like Dorothy Parker, my round table... my Algonquin Hotel. The men I worked with I knew would reappear again—even then taking mental notes—trying to construct a narrative of the chaos of my life.

Part 8: The Paris Theatre, The Fens

The long days of unemployment. At the Paris Theatre—midweek matinees, mad housewives pleasuring themselves with Milk Duds—the iconic man in a trench coat, comb-overs, plastered with plastered heads, mumbling into their greasy sleeves... but that lovely envelope of dark—perhaps a first run Woody Allen—the broad cityscape, served up with King Oliver or Gershwin... things seemed to make sense. My life, maybe at one time will have a similar symphony. Later, below in the Boylston St. Station, a graveyard of old trolleys—a panorama of orange rust. I was a straphanger then—sacrificing my seat for an old gent—my strange dance—a bump and grind—a transit Tango with the other passengers. Eyes averted our forced intimacy when the train stopped suddenly, my joyful collision with a buxom blonde. Late at night—walking through the Fens to Park Drive—a residue from the Ramrod Room—men having trysts behind trees—fertilizing the community gardens with their seed... before the plague.

Part 9: McLean Hospital

First night on the psychiatric ward—he called me his finest creation. I was responsible for the thunder and rain outside—the snapshots of light that popped at the windows—checks on the quiet rooms—museum windows of mental illness—peep shows—all those colorful pink papers—the legal confetti that led them here. A woman took a drag on her cigarette—hollow and sunken chest filled—a woman of substance, until she exhaled. I remember she once grabbed a beautiful young male attendant—squeezing his body close to her—as if she was trying to capture something—his youth—the shock of blonde hair—his strong, undefeated body was now in her reach. An old Boston Brahmin, haughty and insane, asked me if there were cockroaches on the unit... I said no. *Good, you must treat them elsewhere,* she replied. She insisted I was the young researcher from the Panamanian League on Newbury Street—and the young woman, on the 11-7 shift ran from her room in the nude—we danced with this frenzied, beautiful sprite at 3AM—and she performed her swan song—now supine, sedated—restraints. And I talked with a young man—he said he had a correspondence with Allen Ginsberg—*I have seen the best minds of my generation destroyed by madness...*

Part 10: Dr. Solomon Carter Fuller

I taught Black History in the South End/ Solomon Carter Fuller Mental Health Center. A Jewish boy from Long Island—they called me *homey*—I thought, *homely*. They said my sorry, sagging ass looked like it had a ton of bricks resting on it—I never thought about this—I made clandestine trips to the men's room, with a hand mirror to check on my ass—they were right. We took them to the pool on the lower floor—one boy swam with a finger in his ear—a phone conversation with the voices in his head—they were pleasant—the boy had a wild, resplendent smile. Walking down Harrison Ave., past Chico's Bodega, bags of pork rinds in the window, lottery ticket addicts milling around, the usual drunk sprawled out under the awning, down from Boone's Farm or Muscatel, walking down past the Shanty Lounge— had dinner at Asmara with my friend Tesfay—large Ethiopian flat breads, with exotic droppings of meat and vegetables. He spoke of revolution— handsome professorial beard—soft spoken, seemed to ponder each word I said—a minister now—back in Africa.

Part II: Harvard Square Cinema

Double features at the Harvard Square Cinema—hot day—hot movie—*Last Tango in Paris*. Brando didn't believe in names—sex with a young Parisian girl—to die on a balcony with the City of Lights as a backdrop—*That's the way to go,* I thought. And where are you, Frank Cardullo?—Harvard Square turns its lonely eyes to you—Cardullo holding court in the back of the Wursthaus, with the cops, merchants, pols. Cardullo, a small man with a large mustache... and I watched him and the others, sipping on my student's special, house dark, a battered memo pad in my back pocket, scribbling notes. At the Tasty, the counterman presided over a greasy grill... called me *Smiley* for my signature frown. He delivered the dogs on a toasted bun—usually with a cornball pun. The Harvard refugees at the Au Bon Pain. Expelled from the academy—for some reason or another. Gravitated like moths around the light of Harvard Yard. Sat with my friend Byron, trust-fund man, graduate of the wards of McLean—he dabbled in Native American crafts—liked to ogle the young girls passing by, called the old ladies *trouts*. George—a scavenger of scraps of newspapers, and gossip of the street—full of news of the supposed scandals at Harvard—joined us, and let us in on the insane, inside dope.

Part 12: Rexall Drugs, Busing Crisis

Working at Rexall Drugs on Boylston Street during the Busing Crisis—blushing when they asked for condoms across the counter—the mad man in the blue blazer—coat of arms—bulging eyes—shock of dyed blonde hair, rushing in and out of the store—looking perpetually shocked—as if he'd stuck his hand in a socket. A long distance flirtation with a cute 18 year old girl at the soda fountain— the smile, and the retreat, the seduction and abandonment, thought I was in a Thornton Wilder play. I heard the owner say: *It is the rich, Jewish liberals from the suburbs that are causing the crisis.* And everything my Bronx, *shtetl*, pale of settlement (Oh how I loved her *kishkas*) grandma said about the *goys* was true. *Well, the Catholic Church has a lot of money too*, I said. And fired the next day—they said I was rude to a customer... a lesson in life.

Part 13: Neisner's, Kerouac, Ginsberg, Etc...

Neisner's... on a break as an assistant manager trainee for a Big L Discount Store—made my way to the Bromfield St. entrance—slopping up corn chowder with cornbread... then down to Barnes and Noble on Washington Street. Glanced at a book—interesting cover—an endless road, with a setting sun—some guy named Kerouac. Then that rush—the possibility that I could hit the same road—leave tracks—leave the tendrils of a straight-laced suburban roots—that voice in me that pleaded for freedom—caged by conformity. I was an addict, injecting myself with *Dharma Bums, Town and Country*—Allen Ginsberg's mother's pubic, gray, rabbinical beard. I sported a Burroughs's fedora—habituating the Café Algiers in Harvard Square—leaving Beat books on the counter of the grocery store I worked in, at Brookline Village—hoping to provoke a discussion with a customer. Wrote stream of consciousness flourishes in my journals—posturing, unapologetic—as if I was admitted to the cabal—still not venturing much past Kenmore Square.

Part 14: Brahmin Woman Descending

Bay State Road—the old woman/shivering in her fur coat on an eighty degree day—crippled, down the brownstone's steps—reluctantly grabbing the hand of a black attendant—now outside her rarefied cocoon. The young Boston University students—preening like young animals in the sun. *Oh, where are the Dutch Elms?* she thinks. Wiped out by some unruly cancer. Her chalk white face—like a death mask—a Frisbee misses her clenched jaw— on such a warm day—a cold shock of comprehension.

Part 15: Jack's Joke Shop

Jack's, near the Common—your first Dick Nixon mask—all jowls, pointed nose, crowned with hate and Watergate. And the subversive Whoopee cushion—slip it on a seat—and hear the old fart clamoring to get up. Oh—and the clock: *No sex Until Six*—and that carnal circle of sixes. And way before you were a Glaucoma suspect—you could laugh as your eyes pop from your sockets on Slinky springs. You were still a boy—laughing at toys—not that far from boyhood joys.

Part 16: Milner Hotel, Chinatown

It must have been near the Milner Hotel, an old fleabag at the time. And I was found out by an old black gent who watched me while I passed. He knew what my sorry ass was up to—how I made a mountain out of a fuckin' molehill, and save my chicken shit walk—the head tilting attitude—for someone who hasn't seen it before, and has time to give a good God damn. And I remember Chinatown—those late night meals at the Ying-Ying—the staccato chatter of the patrons—the roast ducks in the windows dripped fat seductively, the Chow Fun, greasy dollops of duck, swimming in broth—thick with noodles. I stared at the flashing neon outside the window, on the rain-slicked street. Rod Serling introduced me: *Have if you will, one Doug Holder…*

About the Author

Doug Holder is the founder of the Ibbetson Street Press. He is the Arts Editor for *The Somerville Times*, and teaches writing at Bunker Hill Community College in Boston, and Endicott College in Beverly, Massachusetts. Holder's work, both poetry and prose, have appeared widely in the small press. He holds an M.A. in English and American Literature and Language from Harvard University, and has published a number of collections of poetry over the years.

www.ingramcontent.com/pod-product-compliance
Lightning Source LLC
Chambersburg PA
CBHW021917040426
42447CB00007B/910